J
B
LAUDER

Epstein, Rachel
    Estee Lauder

D0900129

APR   2003

ESTÉE LAUDER

Beauty Business
Success
by Rachel Epstein

A Book Report Biography
FRANKLIN WATTS
A Division of Grolier Publishing
New York / London / Hong Kong / Sydney
Danbury, Connecticut

Cover illustration by Alan Reingold, interpreted from a photograph by ©
Archive Photos/Tom Gates

Photographs ©: AP/Wide World Photos: 73 (Richard Drew), 37, 52, 67;
Archive Photos: cover (Tom Gates), 20 (Morgan Collection), 55 (Russell
Reif), 13, 30, 59; Corbis-Bettmann: 49 (Gianni Dagli Orti), 62 (Kevin R.
Morris), 2, 33 (UPI); Corbis Sygma: 69, 93 (Gregory Pace), 44 (Les Stone),
54; Liaison Agency, Inc.: 74, 97 (Abolafia), 42 (Evan Agostini), 81 (William
Coupon), 10 (Porter Gifford), 84 (Jordan); Photofest: 23, 40; Superstock,
Inc.: 27 (Jack Novak); The Image Works: 87 (Richard Lord).

Visit Franklin Watts on the Internet at:
http://publishing.grolier.com

Library of Congress Cataloging-in-Publication Data

Epstein, Rachel.
Estée Lauder / Rachel Epstein
 p. cm.—(A book report biography)
Includes bibliographical references and index.
 Summary: A biography of cosmetic entrepreneur, Estée Lauder, from
her days of selling face powder at card parties to the present multimillion
dollar beauty company that bears her name.
ISBN 0-531-11705-7 (lib. bdg.)   0-531-16492-6 (pbk)
 Lauder, Estée—Juvenile literature. 2. Estée Lauder, Inc.—History—
Juvenile literature. 3. Cosmetics industry—United States—Biography—
Juvenile literature. 5. Businesswomen—United States—Biography—
Juvenile literature. [1. Lauder, Estée. 2. Businesswomen. 3. Cosmetics
industry. 4. Women—Biography.] I. Title. II. Series.

TP983.A66 E67 2000
338.7'66855'092—dc21
[B]   99-086490

CONTENTS

ESTÉE LAUDER

INTRODUCTION

If you walk into the main entrance of an **upscale** department store in your town, Estée Lauder will probably be the first name you see. Whether it is Saks Fifth Avenue or Neiman Marcus, Lord & Taylor or Macy's, Dillard's, Dayton-Hudson or Bloomingdale's, Estée Lauder products are prominently displayed. And the creams and colors bearing the Estée Lauder name are only one part of the picture. The Estée Lauder Company also makes products labeled Clinique, Prescriptives, Origins, Bobbi Brown, M•A•C, jane, Aramis, and Aveda.

The people who buy these products are not doing anything new. In ancient China, India, and Egypt, women "painted" their faces as a sign of their position in society, as part of religious rituals, to show that they were sexually mature, or to be more attractive to men. Creams to make the

Getting a makeup lesson at the
Estée Lauder Spa at Bloomingdale's

skin feel good go back to the Greek physician
Galen, who lived in the second century. He made
them from water, beeswax, rose petals, and olive
oil—ingredients often used in some modern
creams. Early in the twentieth century, women
used cornhusks to smooth out their skin, and face
powder made from carrots and beets to give them
rosy cheeks. What is different now is that such
products are more likely to be made in a laboratory than grown in the backyard, and they are sub-

ject to safety regulations in the country where they are made or sold.

When Estée Lauder, the woman—yes, there is a real woman named Estée Lauder—founded Estée Lauder, the company, she had no idea it would grow to be so big. But she knew that she loved to make women look beautiful, that she had a talent for selling, and that she was willing to work hard in order to succeed. This book is the story of her life and her company.

CHAPTER ONE

EARLY LIFE

Estée Lauder once told a magazine reporter that her mother was a glamorous, rich, and beautiful woman from Austria who traveled from one luxurious European spa to another pampering herself. She added that her mother was so concerned about her appearance that she never went outside without gloves and a parasol to avoid the brown spots and wrinkling caused by the sun. She said her father was a horseman who was close to Czechoslovakia's royal family, and that they all lived in a big house with a chauffeur and horses. In the beauty business, glamour sells products. The models, the ads, the packaging, and the parties connected with cosmetics all help create an image that customers, in some remote corner of their minds, expect to be part of when they buy the products. Because she was in the beauty busi-

Looking almost like royalty, Estée Lauder poses in her New York town house.

ness, Estée Lauder invented a glamorous past for herself. The truth is that Estée Lauder's parents were not glamorous, but what they gave her is much more important than glamour. Estée Lauder had the self-confidence to become a successful businesswoman as well as a respect for family life that has kept the Lauder family together for three generations. Today, Estée Lauder's children and grandchildren run important parts of the business...and they *do* lead glamorous lives!

Estée Lauder's background was nothing to be ashamed of, though. By the time she wrote her autobiography, *Estée: A Success Story*, in 1985, 15 years after that magazine interview, she came much closer to telling the truth. That book and *Estée Lauder: Beyond the Magic* by Lee Israel together give an accurate picture of her early life.

Estée Lauder was born Esther Josephine Mentzer in 1908 in her parents' home in Corona, Queens. At that time, Queens, a part of New York City, was a rural area. Her mother came from Hungary to the United States in 1898 with five children. Her mother's first husband, who had immigrated earlier, either died or disappeared and was not at the boat to meet the family. Esther's mother married Max Mentzer, who also came from Hungary. The Mentzers had four children together, but two died in infancy. The other two were Esther and her younger sister Renee. Both of Esther's parents were Jewish. Max Mentzer was a tailor. He made clothes for men and women. Later, he opened a hardware store in Corona and the family lived in an apartment over the store.

Esther attended public schools in her neighborhood with other children from Jewish and Italian immigrant families. She was a good and well-behaved student who hardly ever missed school. After school she often helped her father arrange the **merchandise** in his store window so that it would look more attractive to shoppers. Across the street from her father's store, her half-brother's wife and her sister ran a much larger store known as "The Macy's of Corona." Esther spent a lot of time in that store too. When she heard her relatives speak to their customers in Yiddish (a Jewish language used in some European countries) or in the Italian of their birthplaces, she learned that it is easier to sell products when you can speak to people face to face. She also realized that a personal touch with customers makes an important difference. And she saw that a woman could be a success in business.

"Business doesn't have a sex."

Estée Lauder has fond memories of picnics

and riding horseback on the land her father owned in New Jersey. She also likes to remember time spent in Minnesota where she lived with an aunt when she was in high school. There was a polio epidemic in the United States and Esther's mother thought she could keep her children healthy if she moved them out of the big city where diseases spread from person to person more easily than in the country. However, Esther's sister Renee did contract polio and wore a brace on her leg until she was 15.

Esther always loved beautiful clothes and enjoyed making people look beautiful. As a child, she brushed her mother's hair to make it shine and admired her mother's attractive complexion. Esther was also impressed by the fact that her mother was ten years older than her father and thought that it was her mother's beauty that allowed her to "catch" a desirable younger man. Her mother probably did not travel from one European spa to another, but she visited the American spa at Saratoga Springs, New York, where she "took the waters" that were supposed to have health-giving properties. Young Esther wanted to leave ordinary, dull Corona, Queens. She dreamed of being an actress with her name in lights on Broadway—or a skin doctor. What made it possible for a little girl from Queens to realize her dreams? In her life as head of Estée Lauder she combined the glamour of acting with skin care. It all began during World War I with the arrival of her mother's brother, John Schotz, in the United States.

CHAPTER TWO

BEGINNING TO SELL

John Schotz was a chemist who worked in a laboratory near Times Square in Manhattan. He made a variety of products, including mud packs, muscle-building cream, freckle remover, and mustache wax. But what Esther Mentzer loved were his face creams for women, which were called Floranna creams in honor of his wife. They included six-in-one cold cream, moisturizing cream and cleansing cream. Do such creams make or keep a woman's skin beautiful? Not necessarily. However, they do create a barrier between skin and air that slows down the water loss which causes wrinkling. They also make the skin feel soft and smooth. In Esther's mind these creams were powerful tools that improved a woman's appearance and gave her more self-confidence. Her belief that every woman can be beautiful if she takes care of her skin and uses cosmetics to look her best was important to Esther's success. She acted on this belief in high school as she applied her uncle's creams to her friends' faces and, as she put it, "gave away gallons" to her satisfied "customers." It turned out that how the creams were presented was much more important than what was in them, however. Esther Mentzer used the creams to build a beauty empire while her uncle died a poor man.

Soon after high school, Esther Mentzer met Joseph Lauter (they later changed the name to Lauder). She was sitting on a swing at her family's summer cottage in Lake Mohegan, north of New York City, when a stranger in tennis clothes called out "Hello, Blondie!" She was so strictly raised that she barely answered his greeting. However, they began dating and were married three years later in 1930, when she was 22 and he was 28. This queen of the beauty industry remembers that she wore lipstick for the first time at her wedding and that her father made her "wipe most of it off."

In 1933, their son Leonard was born. Although this is the actual date of his birth, Esther Lauder always preferred to keep her own age a secret, so at times she had to say that Leonard was younger than he actually was. Otherwise, people might have figured out her real age! Once questioned about his age, Leonard

Joseph and Estée Lauder

answered, "My age? I'll have to ask my mother. Every time she gives a different interview, I'm a different age. I'll check on what I am this week and let you know."

"My age? I'll have to ask my mother."
—Leonard Lauder

Esther Lauder was not happy in her marriage, though, and in 1939 she divorced Joseph Lauder on the grounds of "mental cruelty." People describe Joseph as a kind man and it is unlikely that he was really "cruel" to his wife, but divorces were difficult to get in those days and claiming "mental cruelty" was a way to get one. The real problem was that Esther Lauder wanted a husband who could give her more social status than Joseph was able to do. He was a man from an immigrant family like hers having difficulty making a living. Also, she wanted to be out and about socializing and selling, while Joseph was happy staying at home with Leonard at night. He was patient, but she was impatient with him.

During the 1930s, Esther Lauder sold her uncle's creams at charity luncheons, card parties, swimming clubs, and resorts. Her customers were middle-class and upper-middle-class Jewish women like herself. Esther's outgoing personality made people like her, and she was careful always to look her best so that other women would want to copy her. Sometimes she sold the creams at a table or booth, but at other times she would just approach a woman and start talking. She began by complimenting the woman on some part of her appearance and then added, "But you could look even better if you would use this cream . . . or that lipstick. Here, let me try it on you." Before the woman knew what was happening Esther Lauder would be applying one of her uncle's products and then complimenting the woman on her improved appearance. She gave beauty lessons as she encouraged her customers to buy something new. Women were fascinated and many bought her cosmetics. Those who didn't, and even those who did, received a tiny free sample to take home—maybe a shaving of lipstick or a few spoonfuls of cream or face powder in an envelope.

Esther Lauder loved making women beautiful—and she was good at it. When she moved into Manhattan in the mid-1930s, she would stop people on the street, in elevators, and in stores and use the same high-powered but friendly approach to encourage them to buy John Schotz's products.

Esther Lauder's real career began when Florence Morris, the owner of The House of Ash Blonde's Salon, complimented Esther on her complexion. Esther went there once a month to "refresh my blondness." Esther told her about the creams and brought them in the next day. Mrs.

Estée Lauder gives a skin care demonstration.

Morris said she would try them when the salon closed, but Esther gently insisted that she would apply them to Mrs. Morris's skin. She put on cleansing oil, then two creams, powder, and something softer than the rouge of the day that she called "glow." Mrs. Morris liked the effect and she liked the way Esther worked. She asked Esther to sell the products at her new shop at 39 East 60th Street, not far from fancy Fifth Avenue. Esther paid Mrs. Morris rent for the counter and kept the money she made selling creams and colors. She changed the name on the jars from Floranna to Estée Lauder, which was the first time she used that name, and put it on labels on black and white jars.

In those days, women spent hours sitting under enormous hair-drying machines in beauty salons. Estée Lauder used that time, when women were usually bored and restless, to apply cream and makeup. The eye shadow she used— there was just one color—was turquoise. She had read that turquoise made the white of the eye look clearer and brighter. The lipstick—also just one shade—was called Duchess Crimson, a color she thought flattered most faces. When she was finished, the women's faces looked as good as their hair did and they were in a receptive mood for buying.

Meanwhile, Estée Lauder was not enjoying

being divorced. Dating was not as exciting as she had hoped. She missed Joseph Lauder and Leonard missed his father. When Leonard got the mumps, he stayed nearby to help take care of him. Estée realized how much she liked being with Joseph, how comfortable they were together, and saw that the divorce had been a mistake. So Estée began courting her former husband again. The two remarried in 1943 and their second son Ronald was born in 1944. But this time, Estée Lauder was determined to be as concerned about her marriage as she was **ambitious** about her business. She would be called "Mrs. Joseph Lauder," not "Estée Lauder," and they would work together as equal partners. Joseph Lauder ran a small laboratory, making the products she had been getting from John Schotz, while Estée Lauder was in charge of sales. This meant getting into more salons and hiring more saleswomen. Estée Lauder was extremely particular about the people she hired. She wanted women who were knowledgeable and looked classy. She made them "try out" at selling as if they were trying out for a play. She rejected anyone who was either too self-conscious or too aggressive. She hired only 1 of the 20 women who first applied, and when her sales force

"Hire the best people and treat them well."

grew she checked up on them every day. Years later, Estée Lauder said her **perfectionism** was an important ingredient in her success.

In those early days of the business, the Lauders worked every day of the week—and almost around the clock. There was a lot of tension in getting orders and then filling them and then making sure they were delivered on time. And Estée Lauder was still trying to be everywhere, touching the face of every potential customer. Those were tough times and she remembers, "I cried more than I ate."

"I cried more than I ate."

The Lauders were starting out at a good time in the cosmetics business. In the 1920s women began rebelling against the Victorian strictness of the 19th century and makeup became acceptable even for "well-brought-up" women. In the 1930s, during the Great Depression, when millions of people were out of work, Estée Lauder noticed that women would rather spend money on face cream than on lunch. And studies made during World War II (1939–1945) found that makeup was good for morale. Even "Rosie the Riveter," who represented women defense workers, wore lipstick and mascara. The United States was prosperous again and more women could afford luxury items like

"I've found the job where I fit best!"

FIND YOUR WAR JOB
In Industry – Agriculture – Business

Even in a machine shop, lipstick and mascara were portrayed as essentials for the working woman.

cosmetics. Also, women were out in the world more, either working or shopping for their families or enjoying themselves. They wanted to look good. Then movies went from black-and-white to color so moviegoers had a better chance of imitating their favorite stars.

Despite these trends, friends and advisors told the Lauders that investing in the cosmetics business was "crazy." They did not listen, though, and in 1946 Estée and Joseph Lauder founded the Estée Lauder Company. They still had only four products—crème pack, cleansing oil, all-purpose crème, and skin lotion, but they changed the packaging from clinical-looking white jars with black lettering to a delicate, pale turquoise. Estée Lauder felt the new jars would add a touch of luxury to most night tables and bathrooms. And Estée Lauder's name was on every jar—right on the glass, not on a label that could fall off if the bathroom got steamy!

After World War II, cosmetics were sold in grocery stores and drugstores, and inexpensive stores called "Five and Dimes," as well as in the more prestigious department stores. Those three kinds of stores are called "mass" outlets where everyone can buy. Department stores are called "class" outlets, which is a shorthand way of saying that only more **affluent** people would be likely to shop there. Estée Lauder knew from the beginning that her products had to be in only the best department stores.

"We are not a budget market, and we know it."

CHAPTER THREE

GROWTH

In the mid-1940s, America's most **prestigious** department store was Saks Fifth Avenue, with a main store across from Rockefeller Center in New York City and branches in many smaller cities and suburbs. Estée Lauder was determined to have her products at Saks. She asked for 12 inches (30 centimeters) of counter space and said it had to be in the front of the store. Since she had no money to advertise, people had to see Estée Lauder products immediately if she was going to make sales. When storeowners talk about "buyers" they are talking about employees who buy what the store sells—not about customers. Saks cosmetics buyers at first turned down Estée Lauder's request. They thought their customers would not be interested in a new and unknown American company, especially since all the fashion excitement in those days came from France. But Estée

Lauder kept going back to the buyers, and refused to accept "no" as the final answer.

One day in 1948, she was speaking at a charity luncheon at the Waldorf-Astoria Hotel, only

Saks Fifth Avenue, New York City

two blocks away from Saks Fifth Avenue. She gave lipsticks to the women at the luncheon and encouraged them to go to Saks and ask for her products. They did just that, and the Saks buyers gave Estée an order. Estée, Joseph, and now teen-aged Leonard Lauder, who was a student at the Bronx High School of Science, worked around the clock to fill it. Many years later, in her autobiography, Estée Lauder wrote about getting into Saks Fifth Avenue. "They were the first, the very first, to take us on and I would never forget it. Ever since, I've had a special place in my heart for this store: breaking that first, mammoth barrier was perhaps the single most exciting moment I have ever known."

"Breaking that first, mammoth barrier was perhaps the single most exciting moment I have ever known."

Store charge accounts were new then—Visa and MasterCard did not even exist. These accounts were almost exclusively at the better stores, which is one of the reasons Estée had these stores as her goal; she knew women were likely to spend more money if they were not limited to the cash in their wallets.

Once in Saks, Estée stopped selling in salons. She sent all of Saks charge-account customers and all her former salon customers an elegant white card with gold lettering telling them that they could now buy her products at Saks Fifth Avenue. And she offered them a free gift of face powder.

The products the Lauders brought to Saks sold out in two days. And this was just the beginning of Estée's truly high-powered career. She began constant traveling and constant speaking —"endless streams, rivers, tides, torrents, oceans of words"—in praise of her products. She was hoping to find "fame and fortune."

After Saks, the next big goal was Neiman Marcus, a chain of luxury stores based in Dallas, Texas. In 1950, despite her hatred of flying, Estée Lauder flew to Dallas and camped out in their buyer's waiting room.

Almost 50 years after she got into Neiman Marcus, Stanley Marcus, the 93-year-old chairman emeritus of the chain, remembers her request. "I asked her," he recalls, "How much space do you need?' She responded, 'That's not important. Four or five feet will do.' 'When can you have your merchandise here?" was the next question. Estée was ready; she had brought it with her. The next day she set it up and was selling at Neiman Marcus. Stanley Marcus remembers that she was stopping everyone who came in the door, saying, "Try this. I'm Estée Lauder and these are the most wonderful beauty products in the world." "It was easier," remembers Mr. Marcus, who is two years older than Estée Lauder, "to say yes to Estée than it was to say no."

Getting in, however,

> "It was easier to say yes to Estée than it was to say no."
> —Stanley Marcus

Stanley Marcus, Vice President of Neiman Marcus, in 1949

was just the beginning. For every new group of stores, and every branch of every group, there was a counter and Estée Lauder had rules to make sure they were successful.

1. Open each store personally and stay for a week. Make sure the salespeople can display merchandise to create an attractive spa-like counter using the turquoise of the Estée Lauder packaging.
2. Select salespeople who are elegant, soft, and refined. Make sure they know how to sell by encouraging a customer to try on products the way she would try on a hat or a dress. Estée did not want salespeople who would oversell the products. (She once heard a saleswoman say, "Estée Lauder's lipsticks never come off," and she turned and said, "Madam, if they didn't come off, I'd be out of business!") And she did not want any "T and T" saleswomen, that is, women who spend too much time on the telephone or in the bathroom (toilet)!
3. Entice the customer with a free gift—almost always a lipstick. Let the customer know about the gift by sending a postcard from the store saying, "Madam, because you are one of our preferred customers, please stop by the Estée Lauder counter and present this card to get a free gift."

4. Draw attention to the new products in town by being interviewed on the radio—(this was before television was a major force) or by the local newspaper's beauty editor.

The idea of a free gift is taken for granted now, but when Estée Lauder began giving things away, it was a **revolutionary** concept and one that was important to her success. She gave samples to saleswomen in other departments, demonstrating how her lipstick matched specific dresses and hats—most women wore hats in those days when they were dressed up—and she gave samples to salespeople in the cosmetics department who sold other brands. These gifts had people throughout the store talking positively about Estée Lauder products.

She also got her products into another Texas chain called Frost Brothers Department Store. While she was opening a store in sweltering San Antonio, near the Mexican border, a Mexican woman approached the new counter and looked longingly at the Estée Lauder jars. She looked totally different from the other women at this fancy store because she was barefoot and had gold teeth that marked her as poor. Estée Lauder was about to ask the woman what she wanted when a saleswoman told her not to waste her time because she *knew* that the Mexican woman would not be buying anything. Estée Lauder refused to listen to the saleswoman. When the Mexican woman pointed to the Super-Rich Moisturizing Crème, Estée Lauder began working on her just the way she would work on any other potential customer—Cleansing Oil, Crème Pack, the Super-Rich All Purpose Crème, and then blush, a drop of powder, and the Duchess Crimson lipstick. The woman looked in the mirror and smiled. Since she could not speak English and Estée Lauder could not speak Spanish, that smile was their strongest communication and formed a bond between the two very different women. The woman then opened her purse, which was overflowing with dollars, and bought two of everything Estée Lauder had used on her. The next day she brought her relatives who did the same thing. It was a good lesson in not pre-judging potential customers.

Since even she could not be everywhere all the time, Estée Lauder came up with the idea of hiring "detail people" to go into the stores unannounced and report on how things were being run. If there was a problem, she herself flew out to correct it. Estée Lauder understood that when you are selling what she called "jars of hope," the merchandising—counter, salespeople, packaging—is as important as the product.

She also was careful to "package" herself to make the best possible impression. She almost

*Estée Lauder and her signature polished look—
complete with veiled hat and gloves*

always wore a black dress designed by the hottest French designer of the day—Christian Dior—and a brown hat with tiny black beads and matching brown gloves. She felt it was smarter to have one or two great outfits to wear whenever she had to make an impression than to have a variety of outfits, none of which looked truly wonderful.

In 1946, the money coming in from revenues, or sales, was the same amount as the money going out: $50,000. By 1960, sales had reached $1 million and profits were probably around $130,000.

Even though she was enjoying some success, Estée Lauder never relaxed her pace. She traveled constantly. Leonard Lauder remembers one year when his mother was away 25 weeks out of 52. She did, however, make a point of telephoning her husband, children, and parents every night when she was away, and because her husband—and a housekeeper—was at home with their sons she knew they were getting good care. She was still trying to apply make-up personally on almost everyone she saw and that led to an Estée Lauder legend. She was on a train going to open a store in Salt Lake City, Utah, when she met a woman who worked for the Salvation Army. This organization helps poor and homeless people by collecting money on street corners, especially at Christmas, and running thrift shops that sell used furniture and clothing. This kind of work is about as far from the glamorous life of Estée Lauder as any work could be, but Estée Lauder found the woman appealing—that is, she found her personality appealing. She did not like the way the woman looked. She said to the woman, "You know, I'd love to make up your face and show you a cream that will make it so lovely to touch."

"Oh, no, thank you," the woman answered, blushing modestly. "Soap and water are just fine for my daily life."

Estée Lauder did not believe that for a moment. She invited the Salvation Army lady to her train roomette, where she applied cream, powder and just a drop of eye shadow and lipstick. The woman looked in the mirror and could not believe the change. Estée Lauder gave her samples of everything and the two women became friends, writing to each other several times a year.

In New York City, Estée entertained store buyers in her office by serving elegant meals catered by the famous Stork Club restaurant a few doors away on East 53rd Street. She always felt that this intimate atmosphere flattered the store executives and made it more likely that they would want to start selling Estée Lauder products. Although Estée Lauder has written that

*Whether entertaining for business or at home, the
Lauder style was unmistakable.*

business is "unisex," this instinct for entertaining was one instance when her femininity was helpful.

In 1958, Leonard Lauder entered the business. He had been interested in it since he was a child. As his mother said, "By the time Leonard was old enough to know what a lipstick was, he was making them." Before he started working full-time, his parents sent him copies of all the company's correspondence when he was away from home. He saw all the notes from stores, memos about deals that were made or lost, and positive and negative letters from customers. Although Leonard Lauder had always seemed extremely interested in the business, his entry into it was not 100 percent certain and the Lauders hoped that letting him in on the details of the big decisions would stimulate his appetite to help them build a large company. He probably would have joined the firm anyway, but the business correspondence certainly helped him make the decision. By 1958 he had graduated from the Wharton School of Commerce at the University of Pennsylvania, done graduate work in business at Columbia University, and served as a supply officer (the closest thing to running a

"By the time Leonard was old enough to know what a lipstick was, he was making them."

Leonard Lauder

store) in the U.S. Navy. He moved on to become president of the company in 1973, when his mother became chairman of the board, and in 1982 he became chairman of the board, the title he holds today.

It was Leonard Lauder's idea to expand to other countries. In 1960, Harrods of London was

Estée Lauder's first international account. Harrods turned out to be as difficult to get into as Saks Fifth Avenue had been 12 years earlier, partly because the first person Estée Lauder spoke to about selling her products in the famous store was the boss of the cosmetics buyer rather than the cosmetics buyer herself. Annoyed, the buyer became determined not to let in this American **upstart**. But gradually, with a media **campaign** in which beauty editors in London wrote about Lauder products—and then had to say the products would

"Persistence is one of the most important ingredients in success."

be sold in England soon without naming a specific store, she made her point. After almost two years, the Harrod's cosmetics buyer relented. Soon after that, Estée Lauder products were also in Fortnum and Mason and Selfridge's, two other exclusive London stores. The United Kingdom was followed by France, Austria, and Canada, and in the early 1960s Estée Lauder opened a manufacturing plant in Belgium to supply the European stores. Italy and Japan soon followed. The man who "sold" Estée Lauder to Japan was Fred H. Langhammer, who is now the highest non-Lauder in the company with the title of president

A busy Estée Lauder counter in Taiwan

and chief operating officer of the Estée Lauder Companies.

Leonard Lauder also made the company's relationships with the stores more formal. By this time, Estée Lauder products were an important brand in the stores where they were sold, so Leonard had negotiating power. He asked the stores to guarantee a year in advance the type and amount of merchandise they would buy, to tell him the location and size of the company's counter space, and the amount of money they would spend on advertising Estée Lauder products. In return he would give the stores promotions, lavish parties held to announce new products; exclusives, promises that only that particular store would be allowed to carry a new product for a certain period of time; and larger payments to salespeople, which are paid by both the store and the cosmetics companies. He was more like his prudent father than his extravagant mother when it came to spending money on the company.

Some of Leonard Lauder's ideas reflected his family background. As a boy, when he went to sleep-away camp his mother used to give him postcards addressed to her so that she could be sure he would write home. Soon after he joined the company he was giving cards addressed to the New York office to salespeople in stores across the country. He wanted to make it easy for them to communicate their suggestions, complaints, comments, or experiences with the people at headquarters.

Leonard Lauder also started a Research and Development Department to make new products that would help make or keep a woman's skin beautiful. However, cosmetics companies must

"Demand the finest quality in product and performance."

walk a fine line between having products that do nothing and products that do too much. If a product actually changes the body's structure or functions by getting below the top layer of skin, then it is no longer a cosmetic but a drug. And drugs are regulated much more strictly than cosmetics by the United States Food and Drug Administration (FDA).

For example, cosmetics are inspected only *after* they come on the market, while drugs are inspected *before* they are sold. Also, cosmetics companies are not required to prove that what they say about the product is true—or even that it is safe—before a product is sold to the public. However, if a cosmetic's safety has not been proved, the label must read: "WARNING: The safety of this product has not been determined." Cosmetics companies are required by the Fair Packaging and Labeling Act to list the ingredients of every product in descending order of quantity. Since water is the main ingredient in most skincare products, it usually appears first on the package. Once a product has been released to the market, the FDA, if it is concerned about the product, must prove that it is either harmful or not properly labeled. If it can do this, the FDA can make sure it is not sold anymore. Cosmetics that claim to actually change the body are regulated as both drugs and cosmetics. Products that are both cosmetics and drugs are dandruff shampoos, fluoride toothpastes, antiperspirant/deodorants, and sunblocking/tanning lotions, including makeup foundations with sunscreen. If the first ingredient listed is called an "active ingredient" then that is what makes the product effective and the manufacturer must prove to the FDA that it is safe and effective before it can be sold.

CHAPTER FOUR

YOUTH-DEW AND CLINIQUE

From 1946 to 1953, the Estée Lauder company grew nicely but in 1953, its growth exploded. The cause of the explosion was a fragrance called Youth-Dew. The fragrance had been used first in a face cream called Estoderme Youth-Dew Crème. It was based on a scent created by Estée's uncle and worn by her mother. Estée Lauder described it as "sweet and warm and romantic, mixing easily with flesh and water." But Youth-Dew did not become a big seller until Estée Lauder added it to bath oil. Before she sold Youth-Dew Bath Oil, Mrs. Lauder tested customers' responses by handing out samples as gifts when women bought other Estée Lauder beauty products.

In 1953, perfume was almost always French, extremely expensive, bought by a man for a woman as a gift for holidays or birthdays, and worn only on special occasions—a little drop behind each ear. French perfumes were so precious and evaporated so quickly that the bottles were sold sealed, often with a cord around the stopper.

Youth-Dew would change all that. Called a Bath Oil, it was meant for every day, just like bathing. Its price of less than $10, when French perfumes like Chanel No. 5, Joy, Shalimar, and *Je Reviens* could easily cost five times as much, put it within the reach of most women and made it

Perfume was considered a treasure in many ancient cultures.

practical to wear every day and to use in large quantities. And the market for Youth-Dew *was* women. Anything written about Youth-Dew stressed that it was a fragrance "made by a woman for women." Also, Youth-Dew had a new time-release formula that made it extremely long lasting ("Like a tattoo," a salesman said recently). And, finally, it was sold unsealed, so the salesperson could encourage a woman to "try on" the fragrance. According to Estée Lauder biographer Lee Israel, while Estée Lauder used to massage cream into a potential customer's face, she now "spritzed" the woman with Youth-Dew. And it goes without saying that she wore nothing but Youth-Dew herself.

What Estée Lauder had envisioned actually happened: women bought—and bought—Youth-Dew. At first they bought the skin products to get the Youth-Dew samples and then they bought Youth-Dew itself. In one Neiman Marcus store, Estée Lauder sales went from $200 a week to $5,000 a week almost overnight. By the mid-1950s, sales of Youth-Dew accounted for 80 percent of the company's revenues. By 1984, the product that had started with sales of $50,000 in 1953 was bringing in $150 million. This came not just from Bath Oil, however. There was also Youth-Dew Cologne, Youth-Dew Perfume, Youth-Dew Hand Lotion, Youth-Dew Deodorant, Youth-

Dew Body Powder, and Youth-Dew Body Lotion. They all eventually came in different sizes to be shaken, spritzed, or smeared on the appropriate part of the body.

Youth-Dew's enormous success was due not only to the product itself but also to the time when it came out. In the 1950s there were fewer brand names and fewer ways to buy products. Catalog shopping mainly meant Sears, Roebuck, and no one had ever heard of the Internet. Today, it seems natural that Gap and Banana Republic have their own fragrances but in those days Gap and Banana Republic did not even exist. With fewer stores and a smaller number of products, it was possible for a new item to make a big impact in a way that is extremely unlikely today. Youth-Dew in the early 1950s was a bit like a new album by Christina Aguilera in 2000.

Estée Lauder wanted Youth-Dew to be sold outside the United States too. In the 1960s, she was trying to interest the buyers of Galeries Lafayette, a well-known and expensive department store in France, but having no luck. After all, the French buyers felt, why would women in France, where perfume was practically a national symbol, want to buy an American scent? Then there was an "accident." Estée Lauder had spilled a bottle of Youth-Dew on the floor of the store's beautiful and exclusive perfume department.

During the commotion, the buyer could see that even French women liked the scent and soon an American *was* selling perfume in Paris.

Youth-Dew put the Estée Lauder Company and its founder on the map in the world of cos-

By the early 1960s, Estée Lauder had become a cosmetics industry icon.

metics. She was now real competition for the other makers of women's beauty products and she was beginning to make real money for herself and her family. With the money they made from Youth-Dew, the Lauders bought their first town house, on East 77th Street—the ritzy Upper East Side of Manhattan.

Youth-Dew was Estée Lauder's first fragrance. In working on it, she discovered that she is what the perfume business calls a "nose." A "nose" is a person who can keep many different chemicals and natural odors in his or her memory and has a feel for a mixture's ability to last, its strength, its evenness, and its appeal. Even when she was no longer actively involved in running the business, Estée Lauder was always consulted when the company was about to introduce a new perfume. Most "noses" do their work in the laboratory. Estée Lauder did that too but she also made her world her laboratory. She would try out a potential new perfume's appeal by wearing it herself and watching the reaction of the people she encountered in the office, at stores, in restaurants, and when she was traveling. She wanted a strong response—positive or negative. If a particular combination got only faint approval or disapproval it was dropped as a possible new Estée Lauder fragrance.

Even though Estée Lauder was thrilled to

White Linen is a classic fragrance loved by women around the world.

learn that she was a "nose," it took 15 years for her to bring out a second perfume. This scent was called "Estée." Estée Lauder says she can actually visualize perfumes, and with this one she was trying for the effect of crystal chandeliers and champagne. Next came Azuree, a fragrance meant to evoke a beautiful young woman lying on a beach on the Mediterranean. That was followed by Aliage, a "sports fragrance," and Private Collection. White Linen, which makes Estée Lauder picture a woman who looks fresh, crisp, and clean,

is her favorite, although she says that the perfumes are like children to her and that she knows
she should not be choosing a "favorite."

The next really big group of products for
Estée Lauder was sold under the Clinique name.
With Youth-Dew, Estée Lauder wanted to change
the way women wore perfume. By contrast, when
Leonard Lauder developed Clinique in 1968, he
saw that women themselves were changing and
he wanted the Estée Lauder Company to be part
of the change.

What had happened between 1953 and 1968
was "the women's movement." Sparked by *The*

A women's protest march on Fifth Avenue in
New York City, 1970

Feminine Mystique (1963) by Betty Friedan, women now wanted different lives. They wanted to do interesting, important work and they wanted to be paid as much as men who were doing the same work. The followers of the movement no longer wanted to spend hours in front of a mirror to please a man, as the "ideal woman" of the 1950s had done. Women were busy and stressed-out and determined to change the world; makeup seemed trivial and time-consuming. And whether they were working or not, women wanted to look more natural and wholesome.

Leonard Lauder thought the company could make products that would match this mood, a line with no extra or unnecessary preparations. He and his mother agreed that the products should be allergy-tested so that they would not set off reactions in women with sensitive skin, yet would still have style—a combination that up to then did not exist. They also agreed that in order to convey the intended no-nonsense message, the products would have to be odorless, or, as they say in the cosmetics business, "fragrance-free." The Lauders also wanted to bring out a complete line of products at one time instead of adding new products every few months or years as they did with Youth-Dew. Clinique was not just a group of related products; it was a system of skin care and color and all the parts had to be in place for it to work.

Estée Lauder selected Carol Phillips, a former managing editor at prestigious *Vogue* magazine, to be in charge of the new line. She had written medical articles in the magazine quoting a dermatologist as an expert on beauty and women's skin. His name was Dr. Norman Orentreich. By coincidence, he was the person the Lauders chose to develop the line, the first time they had involved a doctor in their planning. The collaboration was a great success.

To ensure that the company's rivals in the ultra-competitive cosmetics business did not find out about Clinique, it was developed in extreme secrecy. In the late 1960s the Estée Lauder Company's main office was on the fourth floor at 666 Fifth Avenue. Carol Phillips worked in a tiny windowless room—almost a closet—at the back of the second floor. When she needed to look at color samples for Clinique's jars and boxes, she had to walk two blocks uptown to the Ladies Room of the St. Regis Hotel where the light was good enough to decide. The code name for the product was "Miss Lauder," so that anyone who heard it would think it was aimed at young women and would have no idea of its scientific appeal.

This secretiveness was necessary, the company felt, to prevent corporate spying. Estée Lauder used the same secrecy when she was developing a new fragrance. The test fragrances, as she writes in her autobiography, never had the ingredients listed on the vials. The ingredients were labeled with a code of numbers or letters that only she and her husband and sons understood. She never gave a perfume's entire formula to the laboratory that was making it either. Instead, when the perfume was 95 percent to 98 percent complete and ready to go from vats to bottles, either Estée herself or a member of her family would go to the factory and add the finishing ingredient.

Estée Lauder's main rival—in her personal life as well as in business—was Charles Revson, the owner and founder of Revlon. In those days, Revlon was sold in major department stores and was definitely competitive with Estée Lauder. She has written that "sophisticated spying equipment was Charles's specialty." He had machines to analyze his competitors' products. Estée sees it as no coincidence that soon after she came out with Estée he came out with Charlie. Also, when the Lauders decided to use a single model exclusively—Karen Graham in this case—Revson began using Lauren Hutton, and he copied Estée's Gift with Purchase idea and then brought out a scientific line called Etherea, after Clinique.

> **"Sophisticated spying equipment was Charles's specialty."**

Charles Revson

Estée Lauder has taken great pleasure in winning out over her competitors. When she wrote her autobiography, Elizabeth Arden and Helena Rubinstein were dead and their companies were in the hands of large drug companies. Charles of the Ritz, Max Factor, and Germaine Monteil—all important brands as Estée Lauder was making her mark—were taken over by other companies. And Charles Revson, whose company remained independent, had died also and been replaced by a man, Michael Bergerac, whom Estée liked and admired.

"Keep an eye on the competition."

All the Lauders looked for a name to call the new line. Finally, Leonard Lauder and his wife Evelyn saw the name "Clinique Aesthetique" in Paris and "Clinique" was born. However, the birth was not without incident. Somehow, despite all the security precautions, a company with a product called Astringent Clinique heard about the new line and said it would sue Estée Lauder for violating that company's **trademark**. Working with a special trademark lawyer, Leonard Lauder met with the head of the company and offered to pay $5,000 for the use of the name. This offer was turned down and finally the Lauders got the rights to the name for a payment of $100,000—an enormous sum at the time.

Clinique products also had to be packaged in a way that would be different from Estée Lauder's blue and gold boxes and jars and would also reflect the new lighter approach to beauty the line promised. Since Clinique was to be marketed as a separate line, its packaging had to be entirely distinct from products bearing the Estée Lauder name. Green and silver, Mrs. Lauder and her staff felt, would be the perfect answer to the blue and gold. The first choice was light-green and silver paper, which Carol Phillips decided to use for treatment products. The next was an all-over pattern of tiny fruits and flowers in muted pastels, called *mille fleurs miniscule.* They decided to use this pattern for Clinique cosmetics. But instead of leaving it as it was, the art department blew up the pattern to make it much bigger, which meant that a different part of a flower appeared in a different position on every package. This lack of conformity was a unique concept and the packaging was extremely appealing.

Six Clinique saleswomen were chosen to train people throughout the country about the Clinique concept, or idea, and how to sell it. The salespeople were well educated and ambitious and had to look healthy and extremely clean.

Clinique was introduced to the public, or "launched," in the language of the cosmetics business, as a total line in September 1968, just as the Lauders had planned. To promote the message that Clinique products were scientifically developed, the sales force wore white smocks like hospital lab coats with green stitching and silver buttons. To look closely at a customer's skin, they carried penlights in their pockets. They also sold the correct product based on information customers fed into a crude "computer." By sliding a silvery button across a pastel box, a customer indicated whether her skin was oily or dry, how often she experienced breakouts, and whether she burned in the sun. That computer is still being used today. The skin picture it describes corresponds with a specific soap, a cleanser, and a moisturizer made for oily, dry, normal, or sensitive

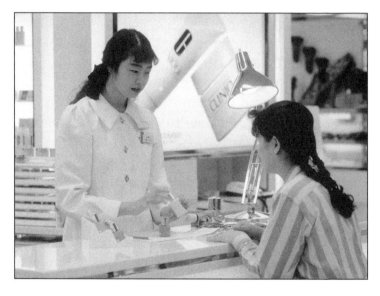

A Clinique saleswoman in Japan tests makeup on a customer.

skin. There are also Clinique lipstick, mascara, and blusher, all wrapped in the light-green marbled plastic cases that debuted in 1968.

Although there was a lot of publicity and excitement about Clinique's debut, most stores were not interested in buying a product they thought would appeal only to women who had allergies. However, the Lauders knew Clinique would appeal to women looking for something new, women who either disliked fragrance or did not want their skin-care and color products to clash with their perfume, and women with fragile skin. It took until 1972 for Clinique to show a profit. By the time Estée Lauder wrote her autobiography in 1985, Clinique's sales were $200 million a year.

One of the reasons for Clinique's success is that, two months after it came on the market, it was made into a company that is related to but also separate from Estée Lauder. Usually, Clinique counters are not near Estée Lauder counters, the products are made in different factories, they do not share staffs, and the idea is for the consumer to believe that Clinique is independent, although Estée Lauder has never denied that it is one of her lines. One reason for the separation was that if the Estée Lauder name were on the package the customer might be confused and not realize how new Clinique was. Another is that if

Clinique's allergy-tested aspect were emphasized as a part of Estée Lauder, it might imply that allergies were a big problem for the original line. And third, Leonard Lauder believed that each company would grow faster if there was a little bit of competition between them.

CHAPTER FIVE

GETTING PEOPLE TO BUY

Estée Lauder's first method of persuading women to buy her creams and makeup was to apply the products on them and give them tiny samples. Her enthusiasm and likeable personality made this an effective way of selling as long as she was hoping only to reach a small number of customers. However, Estée Lauder had no intention of remaining a small seller, so she had to reach out beyond the people she could actually talk to and touch.

Her first plan, shortly after the company was formed in 1946, was to approach some of the big advertising agencies in New York about an ad campaign. She soon found that the $50,000 she could spend was not enough for a prestige firm to take her account. Instead she used that money for more samples, which she called Gift with Purchase—something new in the cosmetics business.

Another way Estée Lauder helped bring her

products to customers' attention was through mailings sent to store charge-account customers. She started with the white and gold card telling Saks Fifth Avenue's customers that Estée Lauder products were now at their store. Then she included advertising messages in customers' monthly bills telling them there was a gift waiting for them at the Estée Lauder counter. Beginning with Youth-Dew, she sometimes enclosed a tiny piece of blotter paper saturated with scent and wrapped in a transparent envelope.

Estée Lauder's first real advertising was done in 1960 in *Harper's Bazaar*, one of the most prestigious fashion magazines. It was a full-page ad for Re-Nutriv, a new face cream with the astonishing price of $115. The ad featured an elegant model and text that asked "What makes a cream worth $115?" The answer was "Rare ingredients. Rare formula. But above all the rare perception of a woman like Estée Lauder who knows almost better than anyone how to keep you looking younger, fresher, lovelier than you ever dreamed possible." The ad went on to list such "costliest" ingredients as turtle oil, royal jelly (from bees), silicone, and leicol, and told how these "youth-giving agents help rebuild and firm the skin, reflecting the freshness and radiance of a years-younger complexion."

In 1962, the Estée Lauder Woman was

"born." She was a model who would appear only in Estée Lauder ads and, because she appeared in every ad, would project Estée Lauder's image of her company and herself. She had classic good looks and was refined and not as blatantly sexy as

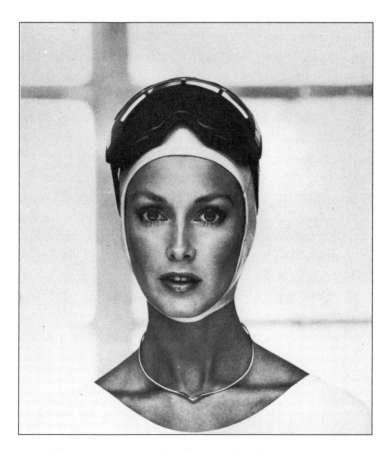

Estée Lauder model Karen Graham in 1974

Estée Lauder judged many cosmetics models were in the early 1960s. From 1962 to 1986 only five different women were used, the most famous being Karen Graham and Willow Bay. In the late 1990s the Estée Lauder Woman was Elizabeth Hurley. These beautiful women wear gorgeous designer clothes and are photographed in settings filled with well-known art, expensive antiques, and sometimes, elegant animals. If they are shown alone, they look as if there would be a dashingly handsome husband and wonderfully well behaved children just out of camera range. Most of the photographs were by Victor Skrebneski, a famous portrait artist. For years the ads appeared only in the most status-conscious magazines such as *Town & Country*, *The New Yorker*, and *Vogue*. In her autobiography, Estée Lauder wrote that many readers requested more information about the clothing and objects in the ads and, "There is a woman in Palm Beach who furnished her home entirely from our advertisements that the owner, herself, calls 'the Estée house.'" Some people even thought Estée Lauder was the model.

The company's most famous ad is the Clinique toothbrush ad, developed in 1974. A toothbrush—and its implied message of twice a day for tooth brushing and twice a day for the basic Clinique skin-care program—had been part of Clinique ads from the beginning. But in this special

Elizabeth Hurley, Estée Lauder Woman of the 90s

ad, the left side of the page featured a giant toothbrush leaning at an angle, bristles on top, in a beautifully clear glass—both the brush and the glass were chosen with great care from close to 100 possibilities. The right side of the page featured Clinique's Facial Soap, Clarifying Lotion, and Dramatically Different Moisturizer with a few words about the simplicity of using them. And over each half of the page was the phrase "Twice a day." The photo was made by Irving Penn, who did many fashion photographs for *Vogue*, and the ads were featured in an exhibit at the Museum of Modern Art in New York. This ad was the opposite of the Lauder Woman ads. "Here the product is the hero," Mrs. Lauder wrote, and it is not identified with any specific age group or life style. Today's Clinique ad has been modified slightly so that instead of a glass the toothbrush alone is leaning on the Clinique products and the soap is being splashed with a stream of water.

Advertising that identified Estée Lauder products with glamour and Clinique's with simplicity made a great deal of sense. However, when Estée Lauder started making products for men it took many years to get the proper image. The men's products were called Aramis, which was a reference to a Turkish root used as an aphrodisiac—something that makes people feel romantic—and also referred to Alexander Dumas's *The Three*

Musketeers, one of whom was called Aramis. Just as Youth-Dew encouraged women to buy perfume for themselves instead of waiting for men to give it to them, Aramis had to convince men to buy expensive toiletries for themselves instead of waiting for women to give them as gifts. Men were accustomed to buying shaving cream and after-shave in drugstores. Vitalis was the only name in men's hair cream. In 1964, when Aramis first came on the market, most men felt uncomfortable in a department store. In fact, the line failed then. But two years later Estée Lauder tried again to get men to wear not only her aftershave and shaving lotion but also Aramis cologne, soap, and Aramis cream to prevent their hands and face from becoming chapped in rough weather. In fact, there was also a plan that gave men lessons in how to take care of their skin. It included such new-to-men ideas as a masque for tightening the skin, pads for refreshing the eyes, aftershave moisturizers, and a special shaving formula for sensitive skin. By 1981, after a number of false starts, Aramis also had an extremely successful and somewhat sexy ad on television featuring Ted Danson, who went on to fame in "Cheers." Aramis, like Clinique, is treated as a separate company under the Estée Lauder umbrella and the name Estée Lauder does not appear on its tortoise-shell packaging.

Samples, bill inserts, advertising, and packaging are all needed to sell cosmetics, which are not something people actually need. Another way is "free ink," a slang term for coverage in the editorial, or non-advertising, part of a magazine or newspaper. The best way

"Tell your story with enthusiasm."

to get "free ink" is to do something newsworthy and make sure that all the editors know about it. The news might be a new product, or a product with a new ingredient. It also might be something about the head of the company, especially if that person is famous like Estée Lauder or Ralph Lauren or Tommy Hilfiger. Estée Lauder has always been excellent at getting "free ink." She spends time "wining and dining" writers, giving them some of the luxury she loves in her own life. She also applies make-up on the women writers, who are flattered by this attention. One writer looked so different after her session with Estée Lauder that her male colleagues did not recognize her when she left the office, and even though it was not her typical look she had to admit she looked better than she was accustomed to looking.

Another method the company uses to generate enthusiasm for its products is a **promotional** event Estée Lauder holds every year near Christ-

At a new product launch, Estée Lauder is joined by singer/actress Liza Minnelli.

mas. This is a time to introduce new products and rebuild excitement about existing products—all aimed at Lauder salespeople, the media, and the general public. When she was in charge, Estée Lauder always chose a theme for these events.

One noteworthy promotional party featured Venice, a city she loves. Art directors went to the Italian island city to find inspiration for new holiday packaging based on rich Venetian colors and elaborate shapes. There was a video featuring famous Venetian sights, including gondolas and niches in St. Mark's Cathedral. The works of famous Venetian artists Canaletto and Guardi were part of the video. To follow up on the theme, the usually blue Estée Lauder counters were draped in Venetian colors of rust and gold and

Charity gala events, such as this one for Alzheimer's, get the Lauder touch.

store mannequins wore Venetian jewelry of beads and glass.

Another promotion involved a request from an old, respected, and now out-of-business New York department store named B. Altman. Estée Lauder helped create an international theme by having booths with beauty experts from Japan, France, China, Germany, and Ireland talking about the makeup secrets of their country. There even was a booth called "America—Fashions in Faces," which gave out American makeup secrets.

A party is another way to get magazine, newspaper, and sometimes even television attention, and Estée Lauder and her company know how to throw a great party. When they introduced Lauder for Men in the early 1980s there was a luncheon at the chic Helmsley Palace Hotel in honor of the "Handsomest Men in New York." The guest list included the governor, people from the society pages, famous lawyers and doctors, actors, and movie stars and even a few members of royal families. The men went home with a napkin sprayed with the line's fragrance and also the elegant menu. But the idea was not just to entice the men who were there to buy Lauder for Men but to get editors to write about the event, and they did. Even the staid old *The New Yorker* magazine covered this party.

A few years earlier, Yves St. Laurent came out with a perfume called Opium. Estée Lauder thought it was a copy of Youth-Dew. She decided to come out with her own competing fragrance. She called it **Cinnabar** and introduced it, after a frenzied rush, only six weeks after Opium had sponsored an extremely successful product launch at Saks Fifth Avenue, Bloomingdale's, and on a party boat in New York Harbor. On the very day of the boat party, Mrs. Lauder announced that she had begun working on a new fragrance two years ago in the south of France. Estée Lauder's launch of Cinnabar took place at the prestigious New York department store, Lord & Taylor. Displays of Cinnabar, oriental-looking orange vases with tassels, which resembled the packaging for Opium, stood at the store's entrance. Models in black-velvet dresses circulated on the first floor, handing out cards for free gifts at the Estée Lauder counter. Saleswomen said that Cinnabar was better and less expensive than Opium and encouraged customers to meet Estée Lauder who was there in person. All the activity—the statements about the product's coming, the sales figures when Cinnabar sold more than Opium, and, of course, the big party at Lord & Taylor—drew a lot of press coverage and made readers all over America eager to try the new fragrance, which almost immediately was outselling Opium.

Packaging is also a way to get customers to buy. The boxes and bottles must look attractive on the counter and also blend with and enhance the owner's decorating scheme. Estée Lauder and her art department are always on the lookout for materials that might be copied. Shells, fabric, Italian tiles, Estée Lauder's mother's silver hairbrush, Evelyn Lauder's cinnabar earrings, and even the lining of an antique book have all served as models for Estée Lauder packages.

The salespeople who work for Estée Lauder in the stores are also crucial in getting people to buy. To make the company's revenues as large as they are, customers who come in for lipstick must often buy other products, such as lip gloss, eyeliner and mascara. This is called "link" selling and it is a specialty of the Estée Lauder Company. This add-on selling must be done gently because Estée Lauder never wants to sell more than a customer feels she needs. In 1998, a reporter from *Fortune* magazine sat in at some sales training sessions and heard these Clinique sales procedures:

CLINIQUE: "What are the words you will never say?"
TRAINEES: "Can I help you?"
CLINIQUE: "Right. 'Can I help you?' makes it sound like we just want to take her money! What should you say instead?"
TRAINEE: "Hello. My name is Tress, I'm a Clinique skin-care expert. Would you like me to assess your skin today?"
CLINIQUE: "Good." Then she demonstrates by

holding up her hand and saying, "Using these three fingers, touch the skin on her face—her forehead, her cheeks, her chin, her eye area—but be sure to ask for permission. Say, 'In order to assess your skin, Colleen, I'd like to touch your skin. Is that okay with you?' Share your observations with her. Bring up her good features before you discuss the trouble spots. Customers may be intimidated, so if you point out one or two things that are terrific, they'll feel good about themselves. 'Colleen, you have such delicate skin, such brilliant blue eyes. Your skin is very smooth, but I can feel a touch of dryness here; have you noticed that yourself?'" The stage is set for the customer to buy the Clinique products that will help correct and enhance her dry skin.

CHAPTER SIX

ESTÉE LAUDER'S LIFESTYLE

Ever since her childhood, Estée Lauder has loved beauty. She loves natural beauty and she also loves the beautiful things that money can buy. After Youth-Dew's success Estée Lauder was a wealthy woman. She soon began going to the fashion shows in Paris and wearing only clothes by famous French designers.

Not long after the Lauders bought a town house on East 77th Street in the late 1950s, they bought homes in Palm Beach, London, Long Island, and the French Riviera. Then Estée sold these houses and bought larger and more fabulous houses in the same areas.

These luxurious possessions are important to Estée Lauder because they add beauty to her life and confirm to her and those around her that she has been successful. It must also be satisfying to remember a time many years ago when she first became a client at the salon of Florence Morris. She complimented a woman on her blouse and said, "Do you mind if I ask you where you bought it?"

The woman smiled as she answered, "What difference could it possibly make? You could never afford it." That woman could never imagine what Estée Lauder can afford now!

Her home in New York City has 25 rooms and is decorated with portraits of Spanish kings, tapestries from Belgium, and upholstery fabric woven for her in Italy. Her home in Palm Beach, which she describes as "open and airy with great light" also has more than 20 rooms. She has written that her house on the French Riviera has a "magnificent" garden designed after the famous garden of French artist Claude Monet in Giverny. And in London her apartment is decorated with English Sheraton and Chippendale antique furniture that she bought in America and brought "home" to England. The wallpaper in her London bedroom is a copy of a blue and white pattern that Thomas Jefferson designed for Monticello, his home in Charlottesville, Virginia. Her Long Island house has tall white columns much like those of Scarlett O'Hara's Tara plantation in *Gone With the Wind.*

When she was interviewed for an article on people who have homes in Florida Estée Lauder was able to put together her love of clothes and décor. She wore a different outfit for each room in which she was photographed.

Estée Lauder's offices have been decorated as carefully and elaborately as her homes. Her first office, which was so small that she used mirrors to

Estée Lauder serves tea in her posh New York office.

make two rooms look like four, had thick dark blue rugs, 19th century furniture, antique Chinese vases, and hand-painted rice paper on the walls. In 1969, when the company moved its headquarters to the GM Building on Fifth Avenue at 58th Street, she added bowls of French beaded flowers, brightly colored porcelain birds, glittering crystal chandeliers, antique gold-finished furniture, and Oriental rugs. She also added a private dining room where she could entertain special guests.

Estée Lauder enjoys not only the good things that money can buy but also the experiences filled with "glamour and excitement." Some of the most spectacular of these experiences are the parties she loves to give. At her parties in New York City and Palm Beach, the women wear long gowns and the men wear tuxedos. There is one waiter for every two people. She serves cocktails on one floor, dinner on another, and after-dinner drinks on a third floor. There is often a live orchestra and dancing as well. Her tablecloths might be gold fabric covered by lace. She has said she expects the same perfection in her parties that she expects in her products.

One of Estée Lauder's most spectacular parties was given to celebrate the opening of an historic Picasso exhibit at New York's Museum of Modern Art in the late 1960s. She painted her tablecloths with colors Picasso used. The plates were the blue of the Mediterranean Sea where Picasso lived. The napkins were an earthy orange color like the rooftops of the French villages in Picasso's paintings. Centerpieces were vases based on the pottery Picasso made and were filled with the French wildflowers he saw while he worked. The menu was a selection of foods that Picasso would have dined on during his lifetime, and the music that accompanied her elegantly dressed guests as they walked around the museum admiring Picasso's art was played by flamenco guitarists popular in the Spain of Picasso's childhood.

Estée loves eating good food at luxurious restaurants—she does not believe in dieting. She also enjoys being with the "right people," men and women who are likely to be doing exciting, worthwhile things at the highest levels of politics, art, or business. They are also likely to be in the society pages, which is where she wants to be as well, both because it gives her social status and because it helps the Estée Lauder Company when she gets "free ink."

Being at or near the top socially was not too hard for Estée Lauder to achieve in New York City, where success in business is recognized and admired and society is quite open to Jews. Palm Beach, however, is well known for excluding peo-

*Surrounded by European dignitaries, Estée Lauder
(second from the left) attends a charity ball.*

ple who have neither social status nor money. It is
also a place with a long history of being particularly unfriendly to Jews, which is called anti-
Semitism. Estée Lauder was persistent about
being accepted here just as she was persistent
about getting her products into Saks Fifth
Avenue. And by a strategy of purchasing expensive tickets to charity events, giving out cosmetics
as favors at those events, holding lavish parties,
and becoming known as an extravagant art col-
lector, she has succeeded in becoming part of the

"in" set there, though not, perhaps, at the top of the social pyramid.

Some of the attention Estée Lauder's lavish lifestyle attracted has not been positive, however. In 1979, two robbers entered her New York town house. They forced her to open her safe, hit her, tied her up along with her maid and her chauffeur, and stole $6,000 and jewelry worth almost $1 million. Mrs. Lauder finally was able to step on the silent alarm that brought the police. After that frightening experience, Estée Lauder no longer publicized her activities and always traveled with a bodyguard.

But glamour and excitement are not the only things Estée Lauder enjoys. Before her husband died in 1983, she loved spending time with him. They used to walk on the beach together, holding hands. She is extremely devoted to her sons, their wives, and their children. She has taken her grandsons to polo matches and horse races and her granddaughters to fancy dinners and Broadway shows. She also enjoys—occasionally—a quiet evening at home watching the news on television.

CHAPTER SEVEN

THE ESTÉE LAUDER COMPANY TODAY

The Estée Lauder Company is vastly different from the organization that Esther and Joseph Lauder founded in 1946. One big change is that the company "went public" in November 1995 and its shares are now sold on the New York Stock Exchange. Another change is the company's size. In 1946, Estée Lauder broke even with $50,000 in sales and the same amount in expenses. In 1998, according to the annual report which all public companies are required to produce, The Estée Lauder Companies Inc. reported sales of $3.6 billion in makeup, skin and hair-care products, and fragrances in more than 100 countries around the world. Most of these countries did not even exist as independent political bodies when the company was founded. In almost every country that sells Estée Lauder products, those with the Estée Lauder, Clinique, and Aramis labels are the first-

The Estée Lauder store front in Warsaw, Poland

or second-biggest sellers in their markets—luxury, allergy tested and fragrance-free, and products for men. Around the world people spend $46 billion to make themselves look, feel, and smell good. Of that total, about one-third, or $16 billion, is spent on the kind of prestige items that Estée Lauder makes, with one dollar out of five going to an Estée Lauder brand. In the United States, The Estée Lauder Companies Inc. has almost half—44%—of the prestige cosmetics business, more than three times as much as its nearest competitor, L'Oréal, which makes Lancôme products.

In addition to Estée Lauder, Clinique, and Aramis, the company makes Prescriptives, a line founded in 1979 offering a wide range of colors to match and flatter more skin tones than Estée Lauder or Clinique. In 1990, the company introduced Origins, which has a natural and ecological emphasis, offering plant-based products in less elaborate, more environmentally friendly packaging. Origins makes items that meet the wishes of young people in the new millennium, including fragrances that are supposed to change the wearer's mood, and scrubbing mitts that make a shower into a massage. They are often sold in their own stores in such youth-oriented places as Cambridge, Massachusetts—the home of Harvard and M.I.T.—and SoHo, which has long been a favorite neighborhood of New York City's young people.

In addition to these "home-grown" products, Estée Lauder sells several brands that were developed by other companies, and are now owned by Estée Lauder Inc. The first "new" company was a Canadian firm called Make-Up Art Cosmetics Limited, which is known as M•A•C. It is described in a recent annual report as selling "color-oriented, professional cosmetics and professional makeup tools targeting makeup artists and fashion cosmetics consumers" and has its own store near the Origins store in SoHo. Next came Bobbi Brown *essentials*, which was founded by

Bobbi Brown, a well-known makeup artist and mother who lives a life that many of her customers can identify with. This line is also aimed at women in the forefront of fashion. Bobbi Brown colors tend to be classic and muted—brownish tones in blush and lipstick. Unlike other Lauder brands, M•A•C, Bobbi Brown, and Origins are sold in hundreds, rather than thousands, of stores.

In 1997, Esteé Lauder Inc. bought Sassaby, Inc., which makes jane, a line of face, lip, eye and nail colors aimed at young consumers, mainly teenagers, with nothing priced over $5.00. Jane is sold in drugstores and grocery stores—more than 12,000 of them—so when the company decided on that purchase it also decided to enter the "mass market" the Lauders had stayed away from for their first 50 years. In 1997, the company also bought Aveda, an environmentally conscious company that does not test its products on animals and has projects that help people in underdeveloped countries. Aveda's main products are shampoos, including its top-selling Shampure, and hair conditioners, but it also sells makeup, body care, and mood-changing aroma products. With this purchase, Estée Lauder has gone back to its beauty salon roots, as Aveda is sold in 25,000 beauty salons, as well as 2,000 Aveda stores. Although this wide distribution would usually make Aveda a "mass-market" product, its high prices keep it in the "class" column. Estée Lauder also makes products bearing the Tommy Hilfiger name, such as "tommy" and "tommy girl" perfumes, as well as the entire line of Donna Karan beauty products. Estée Lauder is also bringing out new ways to sell cosmetics. Building on the "computer" idea that it began in 1968, Clinique opened a web site in 1996. And now Estée Lauder, Clinique, and Aramis have pioneered in a concept they call "free play," which allows a customer to choose from an enormous array of products that are in front of, rather than behind, the counter and do not require the assistance of a salesperson for testing. The company has realized that in these days of independent women—and men—makeup customers are likely to have their own ideas and to be well informed and thus appreciate this freedom. When Estée Lauder began in the cosmetics business, her personal touch meant a lot to her success, and now that her touch is no longer available, the company is giving customers the fun of touching their own faces . . . before they buy!

The company has also been branching out from its department-store roots. In addition to Origins stores, there are also Estée Lauder stores and Clinique stores, and Clinique is now sold in some college bookstores.

In important ways, however, the company has not changed. Although The Estée Lauder

Companies Inc. sells stock to the public, three-fourths of that stock is owned by the Estée Lauder family. Leonard Lauder, Estée Lauder's older son, is chairman and chief executive officer of the company and his younger brother Ronald S. Lauder is the chairman of Clinique Laboratories, and Estée Lauder International, which is responsible for 43 percent of the company's revenues. Leonard Lauder has been involved in the business since he was a teenager, when he used to make deliveries on his bicycle. He joined the company in 1958 and has been there ever since. In a 1998 interview in *Fortune* magazine, Leonard Lauder revealed how much he is like his mother when he said, "'Every time I talk to our people, every time I go to a sales meeting, every time I meet with beauty advisers, I say to the people, 'Listen, I simply want this to be the best company in the world. And being the best means being the best. Being the best sales, being the best profits, being the best products, being the best advertising, being the best people,

"At the office, the name of the game is Lauder."

"Listen, I simply want this to be the best company in the world."

being the best everything.'" The lesson of perfectionism was not lost on Leonard Lauder.

Ronald Lauder, unlike his older brother Leonard, has done many things in addition to working at Estée Lauder. He is interested in politics and has been deputy assistant Secretary of Defense for European and NATO policy, U.S. ambassador to Austria, and candidate (unsuccessful) for mayor of New York. After his mother was robbed he wrote a book called *Fighting Violent Crime in America* in which he outlines a plan for using the advanced technology used by his business and other successful businesses to help reduce crime. Ronald Lauder now runs the Ronald S. Lauder Foundation which is working to revive the Jewish life in Eastern Europe that was almost destroyed by the Holocaust and Soviet Communism. The Foundation supports schools and summer camps in the former Soviet Union, Poland, Hungary, Lithuania, Germany, Slovakia, and Bulgaria. In 1999, he was elected president of the prestigious Conference of Presidents of Major American Jewish Organizations.

Leonard's wife Evelyn is senior corporate vice president of the company. Three of Estée Lauder's grandchildren are also in the business. Leonard Lauder's son William, who had been the head of Origins, is now president of Clinique Laboratories Inc. Ronald Lauder's daughter Aerin Lauder Zin-

*Ron Lauder with daughters Aerin (left)
and Jane (right)*

terhofer is the director of product development for the Estée Lauder brand, and his younger daughter Jane helps to direct the Clinique USA sales force. Gary Lauder, Leonard Lauder's other son, is not in the business. He works in Silicon Valley, California, encouraging new high-tech companies. The other members of the family live within a few blocks of one another on New York's Upper East Side, near Estée Lauder's home.

The family has continued the company founder's interest in art and beauty; Leonard Lauder heads the Board of Trustees of the Whitney Museum of American Art and Ronald Lauder holds that position at the Museum of Modern Art. Along with the Guggenheim Museum, these are the three most prominent modern art museums in New York City—and possibly the world. Evelyn Lauder, who suffered from breast cancer, has been active in establishing The Breast Cancer Research Foundation, which fills gaps in medical-research funding. In October, which is National Breast Cancer Awareness Month, customers who visit Estée Lauder, Clinique, Prescriptives, Origins, and Aramis counters obtain pink breast-cancer-awareness ribbons and informational bookmarks. These divisions of the company also donate money from selected products to the foundation.

Joseph Lauder died in January 1983, as the Lauders were preparing to celebrate their 53rd wedding anniversary. Mrs. Lauder was devastated and stopped working for a while, but within a few months she was back at her desk advising the company on a new perfume.

In 1994, Estée Lauder broke her hip. She has not appeared in public since then.

CHAPTER EIGHT

SUCCESS

Estée Lauder called the autobiography she wrote in 1985, *Estée: A Success Story*. In it she shares some of the secrets of her success, which she calls "Lauderisms." They are:

1. Find the proper location for your counter, which is to the right of the entrance because that is how people's eyes wander, and make sure you have enough counter space to make an impact.
2. When you are angry, never put it in writing.
3. Remember that you get more bees with honey and never pull out of a store, even if you are not being treated well. This ensures that there will be no rumors that you pulled out because you were not doing well at the store.
4. Keep your own image straight in your mind.

*Estée Lauder's elegance and grace were
still evident in the 1990s.*

She goes into detail on this, writing, "From the beginning, I knew I wanted to sell top-of-the-line, finest-quality products through the best outlets. If I were to sell our cosmetics at discount stores, our sales would pick up for a brief time, and then decline dramatically. We are not a budget market, and we know it. The woman who buys the best (not always the most expensive, by the way) is reassured by finding the best where she expects it to be. Our credibility would be harmed if we cheapened our image."

5. Keep an eye on the competition.
6. Divide and rule. Give people in the company responsibility but keep Lauders in charge. "At the office the name of the game is Lauder, imperial as that may sound. Running a business is rarely a matter of group vote."
7. Learn to say no.
8. Trust your instincts and common sense; they are more reliable than surveys.
9. Act tough; don't give in. Persistence is one of the most important ingredients in success. It comes from believing in yourself.
10. Acknowledge your mistakes. Some that she mentions are: false eyelashes, going after the teenage market (this was before the purchase of jane), and trying a hor-

"You are allowed to make the same mistake ... once."

mone cream. "You are," she cautions, "allowed to make the same mistake . . . once."

11. Write things down.
12. Hire the best people and treat them well.
13. Break down barriers between people; entertaining them, especially with food, often works to do this. She particularly likes entertaining on a small scale in her office.
14. Give credit where credit is due. Remember birthdays, holidays, and anniversaries.
15. Train the best sales force.

"Finally, remember that the same principles that contribute to business success apply equally to women as they do to men. Business doesn't have a sex. Demand the finest quality in product and performance. Tell your story with enthusiasm. Always look for things that should be changed. We learn too much, every day, to be satisfied with yesterday's achievements."

Success has come to Estée Lauder not only in the form of a large and respected business but also in the form of honors given by philanthropic, civic, and industry groups. In 1977 she was given an award by the Association for a Better New York for her donation of three adventure playgrounds in Central Park. Two years later, she received the Gold Medal of the City of Paris ". . . not for any single accomplishment, but simply what she stands for, what she is, her singular genius." In 1968 she was given the Spirit of Achievement Award by Albert Einstein College of Medicine of Yeshiva University in New York City. In 1967 she was named one of the Ten Outstanding Women in Business in the USA by a group of business and financial editors. Her numerous cosmetics industry awards include The American Society of Perfumers Living Legend Award in 1994, the same year that Youth-Dew received the Fragrance Foundation's FiFi Award for Perennial Success, celebrating 40 years of popularity. She was also, in 1993, the first person ever to be awarded The Neiman Marcus Award for Distinguished Service in the Field of Fashion for the second time.

In 1998, *Time* featured Estée Lauder as one of the 100 "Most Important People of the 20th Century."

Now in her 90s, Estée Lauder can look back at a life with more success than even *she* dreamed possible when she was a young girl growing up in Corona, Queens. Through her products she has touched women and men in every corner of the world. She can look with pride at her productive children and grandchildren. There has never been any scandal connected with her life or the lives of her family, which is unusual in the beauty and fashion industry.

When she thinks about her accomplishments,

she realizes they were not easy. But she never says that it was anything special about her that made them possible. She attributes her success to hard work, persistence, and perfectionism—qualities she feels other people can copy. She would like to inspire them to do so.

1908	Esther Josephine Mentzer is born in Queens, NY.
1915	Her uncle, chemist John Schotz, arrives from Austria.
1930	She is married to Joseph Lauter (they changed the name later).
1933	Leonard Lauder, now chairman and chief executive officer of Estée Lauder, is born.
1939	Estée and Joseph Lauder divorce.
1940 (?)	Estée Lauder opens first counter at the Florence Morris salon, a beauty parlor on East 60th St., New York City.
1943	The Lauders remarry.
1944	Ronald Lauder, now active in the company and many political organizations, is born.
1946	The Estée Lauder Company is formed.
1948	Estée Lauder products are accepted for sale in Saks Fifth Avenue.

1953	Youth-Dew Bath Oil makes a big splash for the company.
1958	Leonard Lauder enters the business on a full-time basis.
1964–67	Line of Aramis products for men debuts, fails, and is reintroduced.
1968	Clinique line of allergy-tested, fragrance-free cosmetics and treatment products comes on the scene.
1968	Estée, the company's second perfume, makes its appearance.
1979	Debut of Prescriptives, a line geared to many skin colors.
1990	Debut of Origins, an ecologically sensitive product line aimed at young people.
1995	Estée Lauder Companies sells stock to the public on the New York Stock Exchange.
1995	Estée Lauder Companies acquires M•A•C and Bobbi Brown *essentials*.
1997	Estée Lauder Companies acquires Aveda, specializing in botanical hair-care products, and Sassaby, Inc., maker of jane, a line of inexpensive color products made for teenagers.
1998	Estée Lauder is named by *Time* magazine as one of the 100 "Most Important People of the 20th Century."

affluent Having plenty of money, property, or possessions

ambitious Full of ambition; eager to succeed

campaign An organized activity to attain a political, social, or commercial goal

cinnabar A red or brown mineral that is the chief source of mercury

merchandise Things that can be bought or sold; commercial goods

perfectionism A tendency to set extremely high standards and to be dissatisfied with anything less

prestigious Having prestige; honored, esteemed

promotional Related to publicity, as for a product on sale

revolutionary Marked by or resulting in radical change

trademark A name, symbol, or other device identi-
fying a product, which is registered with the
government and legally restricted to the use of
the owner

upstart A person who has become arrogant or self-
important because of his or her success

FOR MORE INFORMATION

BOOKS AND ARTICLES

De Castelbajac, Kate, *The Face of the Century: 100 Years of Makeup and Style*, New York, Rizzoli, 1995.

The Estée Lauder Companies Inc. *The Annual Report for 1996-99*, 767 Fifth Avenue, New York, NY 10153.

"Estée's Heirs," by Cathy Horyn in *Harper's Bazaar*, September 1998.

Israel, Lee, *Estée Lauder: Beyond the Magic*, New York, Macmillan Publishing Company, 1985.

Lauder, Estée, *Estée: A Success Story*, New York, Random House, Inc., 1985

"Why Women Find Estée Lauder Mesmerizing," by Nina Munk, *Fortune*, May 25, 1998, New York.

ORGANIZATIONS

Cosmetic Executive Women
20 East 69th Street, 5C
New York, NY 10021
212-717-2415

Cosmetic, Toiletry and Fragrance Association
1101 17th Street, N.W., Suite 300
Washington, D.C. 20036
202-331-1770

Fragrance Foundation
145 East 32nd Street, 14th floor
New York, NY 10016
212-725-2755

INTERNET SITES

The Estée Lauder Companies, Inc.
http://www.Elcompanies.com
This site provides a company history and information about the "Pink Ribbon Breast Cancer Awareness Campaign." From here you can click over to web sites of specific brands such as Clinique, Tommy Hilfiger, and Aveda.

The Food and Drug Administration
http://www.fda.gov
Read about cosmetic safety, animal testing, aromatherapy, tattooing, cosmetics and teenagers, and more.

INDEX

Page numbers in *italics* indicate illustrations.

ABOUT THE AUTHOR

Rachel Epstein lives in Brooklyn Heights with her husband in an apartment overlooking the canyons of Wall Street where he works as a lawyer. She has two grown children both of whom are working on doctoral degrees in history. Rachel has written a business dictionary called *BizSpeak* and books for children and teenagers on finance and health, including a book on the eating disorders anorexia and bulimia. She has also written children's biographies of W. K. Kellogg, who founded the enormous cereal company, and Anne Frank, who perished in the Holocaust. As an outgrowth of writing that book, Ms. Epstein is now a Gallery Educator at the new Museum of Jewish Heritage/A Living Memorial to the Holocaust in lower Manhattan, right across from the Statue of Liberty, where she teaches school groups about Judaism and about World War II. She is also involved in fund-raising for Jewish groups that help people all over the world who are in need or in political trouble. From 1989 to 1994, she wrote a weekly column on shopping for *The New York Observer*. In addition to her serious pursuits, Ms. Epstein loves to shop and she loves makeup!